Diamond D

The One in a Million Girl

LuLu Ferrari

Illustrated by Arta Gashi-Loxha

DEDICATION and ACKNOWLEDGMENTS

THIS BOOK IS DEDICATED TO THE REAL DOLORES.

SHE WAS *ONE IN A MILLION* BECAUSE OF HER *KINDNESS*.

DOLORES, YOU WERE *GIVING, CARING, AND FULL OF LOVE*. YOU BROUGHT *LAUGHTER* TO EVERYONE.

I THANK YOU FOR OPENING UP MY EYES TO ALL OF THOSE THINGS AND SHARING YOUR WORLD WITH ME.

OUR JOURNEY TOGETHER WAS *MAGICAL*. I WILL ALWAYS LOVE YOU.

SPECIAL THANKS

I HAVE BEEN FORTUNATE TO HAVE SO MANY SPECIAL PEOPLE WHO ENCOURAGED ME WHILE WRITING THIS BOOK.

I'M BLESSED TO HAVE YOU IN MY LIFE.

OLIVIA KRESSER, THANK YOU FOR ALL YOUR SUGGESTIONS; THEY INSPIRED ME

MILO KAUFFMAN, THANK YOU FOR YOUR CREATIVE THOUGHTS

KARA RICCIARDI-LOFRANO, THANK YOU FOR YOUR IDEAS AND MANY PHONE CONVERSATIONS

THE NUNEZ FAMILY~ JEN, JEFF, JEFFREY LUCA, JAYDEN, AND JIANNI

THE BARBIERI FAMILY~ JULIA, CHRISTINA, DAWN, TOM, AND SABRINA SCIRE

THE KAUFFMAN FAMILY~ MINA, JEFF, MILO, AND CALVIN

THE DAMASHEK FAMILY~ JESSE, ANDI, JACK, AND MAYA

DR. DEBBIE AND MR. STEVEN GLASS

THE GUIDO-DESIMONE FAMILY~ MARIA RAY, PATRICK, FRANK SIMON, RAFAELLA, AND VIRGINIA

MARIA GRIFFIN, WENDY GU, KAT IRANNEJAD, TONY KEEVAN (RIP), DEIBE RONDON

CHELSEA HORENSTEIN, CARLA DAICHMAN, TOBY KLEIN

KATIE AND JEN RUDOLPH, ARLEEN MAIORANO, RACHEL ASCHELEW

TINA CASTELVETRE, SOPHIA TENKLEY

This Book ◆ Belongs To

_____

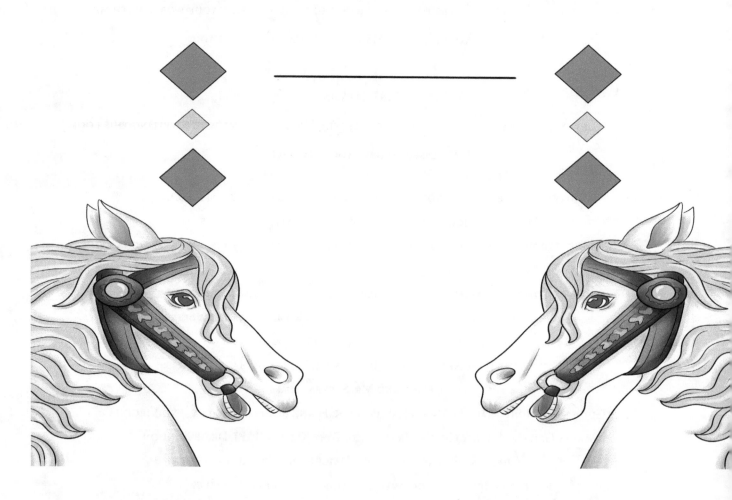

On a sunny spring day, a little girl named Dolores is born!
Her mother and father are amazed to see she has a
beautiful, extraordinary, diamond-shaped birthmark on
her cheek.

They are overjoyed with happiness in how special she is
and say, "She is one in a million!"

Dolores is kind, friendly, and helpful, and with her unique diamond-shaped birthmark, everyone who meets her thinks she is one in a million, too!

If she finds a lost kitten, she brings it with her mom and dad to the animal shelter where her mother volunteers.

At school she helps her friends with their art projects, reading, and math.

A a B b C c D d E e F f G g H

Dolores ☆
Lucy ☆
Milo ☆
Julia ☆

$$\begin{array}{r} 1 \\ +\ 1 \\ \hline 2 \end{array}$$

All the girls and boys like her because she is so much fun
and kind. Today, there is a soccer game. Dolores is
running very fast and makes a goal for her team.

Everyone cheers!
Then Dolores makes a goal for the other team!

The game ends in a tie.

Afer the game, Dolores shares healthy snacks from her red wagon.

Later, there is a lot of excitement at the park! The children are laughing and talking to Dolores. Julia is curious and asks about the special mark on her cheek.

Milo also wonders and asks, "What is that diamond shape? Is it a sticker?"

Christina asks, "Is that diamond shape a tattoo?"

Lucy, Dolores' best friend, excitedly shouts...

"No, no, no!

The diamond shape on her cheek is her

special birthmark!"

Milo says, "Cool! I like it!" "Oh, wow," says Julia, "It's pretty. I wish I had a diamond birthmark."

Lucy turns to Dolores and says, "I think we will call you DIAMOND D!" Milo says, "Diamond D, you are so lucky! You are one in a million!"

Diamond D made new friends that day, but now it is time to go home. "See you soon," Diamond D calls to her new friends. "Bye-bye, Diamond D!" all her new friends shout back to her.

Diamond D lives in Brooklyn, New York, up, up, up high in The Clocktower building.

The next day, Diamond D rides the carousel with her very best friend, Lucy.

Riding on her favorite horse, she loves to watch the boats gliding under the Brooklyn Bridge.

Diamond D likes to imagine
where they might
be going...

At night, Diamond D's mother comes to tuck her into bed. "Look, Mommy!" Diamond D says, "The lights on the bridge make the river shine and look like a mirror!"

Diamond D's mother says," I see, and it makes the skyscrapers look like they are dancing against the sky, too!"

The next day, Diamond D invites three friends to The Clocktower for a play date to draw. She shares her big, blank drawing pads and her colored pencils.

Milo shows his drawing of the moon with its arms wrapped around the Brooklyn Bridge. Everyone takes turns sharing and clapping for each other's artwork.

"I like how you drew the moon and the bridge,"
Diamond D says to Milo.
Milo says, "Oh, thank you."

"I like the colors you used for the buildings and the river, Julia," Diamond D says. "Lucy, I like how nicely you kept our pencils together so they don't get stepped on."

Julia and Lucy both smile and say, "Thank you."

Diamond D's friends love visiting The Clocktower for another reason. HOBBY! Hobby is Diamond D's Old English Sheepdog. He is really big for a puppy and likes children.

Today, Hobby has a special job. He is bringing cookies to Diamond D and her friends!

Excitedly, Diamond D says, "Did you see his eyes? Hobby has one blue eye and one purple eye!"

"Hey!" says Milo, "Hobby must be one in a million, too!"

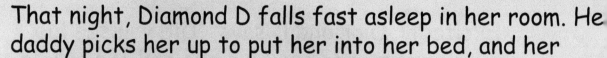

That night, Diamond D falls fast asleep in her room. He
daddy picks her up to put her into her bed, and her
mommy and daddy both kiss he
on the cheek. Then mommy
whispers, "Now it's time
to plan our little girl's
7th birthday party."

About the Author

This is my first children's book. I was inspired to write this book because my partner, Dolores, was an exceptional person in my life. She exemplified kindness, giving, and happiness. She taught me so much about love, friendship, and cultivating relationships in one's life. I was blessed to share my life with her for 20 years. She was One in a Million to me and to all who met her. Writing this book was a joyful experience and a fun carousel ride for me!

Lulu Ferrari lives in Dumbo, Brooklyn New York.

For YOUR invitation to Diamond D's 7th Birthday Party, go to DiamondAndHobby.com

Printed in the USA
CPSIA information can be obtained
at www.ICGtesting.com
LVHW081804141223
766217LV00007B/529

9 781955 794008